As If It Were Visible

Poems

Sharon K Sheppard

Sharon K. Sheppard

for
Vangie and Terry
Bruce, Kate, Eva, and Ella

Also by Sharon K Sheppard
All We Ever Wanted © 2013

Table of Contents

Acknowledgements

Many thanks to friend and fellow poet Dave
Healy, who once again waved the publisher's
wand over my poems and materialized a book.
How on earth does he do that?

Thanks also to those who cheered me on with the
first book, practically guaranteeing that there
would be a second . . . particularly friends from
my two poetry groups, my art group, and my
sister-in-law Carmen, whom I lovingly refer to as
my "agent."

And a very special thanks to readers because, after
all, sharing it with you is the whole point.

"The moment you doubt whether you can fly,
you cease forever to be able to do it."

J. M. Barrie, *Peter Pan*

Introduction

When I was a child, I watched the play "Peter Pan" with my brother Gary. It utterly convinced me that I could fly. Hadn't Peter Pan done so before my very eyes? Hadn't he said that all I need do is think happy thoughts and up I would go? Life, of course, eventually set me straight about the law of gravity, and what was really possible. I had to come down to earth like everyone else. But, I have to admit, I still dream of flying.

Writing poetry and flying have more in common than one might think. In order to fly, one must temporarily abandon what we see as 'reality' and trust in possibility. Flying is the very soul of freedom, and writing poetry requires a certain freedom. And so, we start with what is, spread wide the wings of imagination, and up we go!

This second book was born of the same close observation and pondering of life that hatched the first book. There is love here, and bewilderment. Awe and curiosity. Sadness and joy. I am very grateful for those who helped create these experiences in my life. I lost two of them to death last year: my sweet mother-in-law Vangie, and my dear friend Terry. This book is dedicated to them, and to my four very special grandchildren, who I hope will carry some part of me into the future. May they never stop believing they can fly.

As If It Were Visible

Poems

Something Much Softer

Before I opened my eyes
I thought how I didn't want to, how
I'd rather stay, counting out dreams
Instead.

Before I opened my eyes
I thought how, maybe today
I'd have-it-out with life, recalculate
My course . . . again.

Before I opened my eyes,
I dreamed snow drifting down
Over the bare blue knuckles
Of the world, softening it.

When finally, I did open my eyes,
The light had come. Snow also.
And I saw how it is not always determination
Which moves us forward,

But something much softer,
Threaded into and through us,
Like the snow-lined rivers of branches
Holding up the sky.

Silence

Sweep and rush of snow,
its crisp floodwaters
folded
into every yielded space;
white heft
of its accumulation
feathering branches, rooftops,
anywhere a foothold
may be found.

Morning after morning
I rise to the pristine
silence,
my imagination blanketed,
an emptiness
overwritten, here and there
by the scrabbled tracks
of some furred and tender
thought
treading the silence
on tiptoes.

Poetry 6 a.m.

Up again. Floundering
Through dark drifts of morning
So deep
The kitchen table lamp
Goes before me, like a lantern.

Feeling lost, I stumble
From one worthy word to another,
Recognizing none
That will fold
Into its papery wings
The pith of my poem
To make it fly.

One Perfect Day

We raised a tent
between two chairs
with a blanket stretched
across their upright backs, and
we lay beneath it, our faces glowing
like phosphorescent ghosts,
flushed in red and green. For hours
we whispered our excitement
at Santa's expected visit
and what the cold white light of dawn
might bring. Long before midnight
our chatter trailed off into sleep,
and who knows what dreams we dreamt
before morning found us, collapsed
into the arms of Christmas, just waking
to the one perfect day
of the year.

The Quilt

She must have sat, her shoulders hunched in light
From kerosene
And squinted, as her thread met needle's eye
Then slipped between,
And...stitch by careful stitch...sewn cloth to bat,
Bound dream to dream.
For, in the leaping colors of its form
She may be seen
To fly beyond the drudge of common days,
Transcending comforts sacrificed, with grace.

In Defiance

For minutes...nothing
but teeming white snowflakes
drifting like down
into the world.

Then, the swift
upward stroke of a chickadee,
in defiance
of all this fluff, shot
like a seed-fueled
rocket
into the trees!

Chickadees

This morning
Chickadees hosted
   A chat fest
      A ribald reunion
         A rollicking riot
In the leafy spaces of the arborvitae.

Their invisible flutterings,
Their tinny snare drum voices
Rattled and tapped inside my head,
Stirring into
My grumpy morning mien
A heaping measure of humor.

Little scalawags!
Little comics with castanets!

Waking on a Winter Morning

It's still dark, and so for a while
everything is possible.
Beyond the brittle stoicism
of glass, there may be crickets
piercing the night with song,
or a dust-winged moth
folding and unfolding, silently
into the treetops.
Perhaps, beyond my seeing,
in some grassy place,
a doe sinks down, eyes wild…sides heaving
as the fawn slides, steamy and damp,
from her body. Is it just possible
that every dreamed-of thing
eventually unfolds itself into the world?

I woke, this winter morning
to visions of spring
stretching itself beneath the snow.
Surely somewhere in this world,
water is shrugging off
its prisons of ice, and flowing forward;
lives benumbed by grief
are letting sorrow
slide from their shoulders;
the lost
are finding their way home.

Today

It rose
Among the dark fingers
    of the branches,
Flaming pearl...pouring off rainbows;
And every stone-cold insinuation
    of January
Melted, and pooled at my feet
As winter's long shadows
    frayed
And disappeared.

Two Snowy Drifts

Whatever it was I saw
Lying stark and white
Against the dark April field,
It was enough for me.

Either, two snowy drifts
Stood mourning the last of winter
Or, two small flocks of gulls
Had gathered to spend the night.

All that matters is this:

In one swift movement,
They lifted away
And swirled into joyous life,
A blizzard of pale grey wings!

One More Time

Yesterday, because it was
long past time to let go,
because I feared the choked sniggers
of my neighbors in passing cars;
I lifted two armfuls of fir boughs,
still green and fragrant, from the
milk cans outside my front door,
and held them to my face
one more time, inhaling
the unmistakable spice of Christmas
before laying them on the trash pile,
and walking inside to wash
the sticky memory from my hands.

One Day

In winter,
I like to remember
How, one day in early spring,
The cottonwoods dipped
Their long waxy fingers
Into a blue-basin sky
And shook,
Into the bark-scented air,
A million feathery seeds
That swirled and danced
Around my body, then piled
At my feet in drifts
Like a warm and generous
Snow.

Questions

What if today
I were to walk down rows of corn
At daylight's edge, and feel the dew-wet leaves
Against my face? Would morning whisper
Life is grace?

And if instead of rushing headlong
Into love's embrace,
I were to sit in quiet contemplation of
The beauty in your face, would evening whisper
Love is space?

And if I paused at midday
In life's solitary race,
To birth a single clarity from out this murky haze,
Would someone whisper,
You are place?

Where It Will Rise

For minutes
before it sizzles up,
I imagine
how it will emerge
from the quicksilver of the waves
just there, beneath the spot
where a slender knife of cloud
fingers up at the horizon, edged
with buttery light. And I smile
at how this waiting and watching
has become my daily bread,
each sunrise, a beginning
uncompromised by doubt,
and wild
as the sea rolling up
at my feet.

Gray

Gray today.
Sea birds quibbling
over nothing
in the wave-nibbled
   forever
of the sand.

Becoming

The dead
are not buried here,
but are left
to discover what joy may be found
in becoming another:
ear bone of whale,
cold blue knuckle of crab, red
elaboration of kelp,
diatom, sponge, sea worm,
the thick green sweep
of wave to shore, a gray
speckled beach
that goes on forever.

High Tide & Windy

O pristine ornamentation!
Delicate little hives
of spume
rising.

A Dolphin

It curves darkly
then disappears into
the silver bundles of water
    so quickly
that I write it off
to illusion   to the purple
underside
of one wave rising
into the gold spangle of dawn
    except
there it is again
where the sea bulges
over hidden berms
of sand
    a dolphin   leaping
in the thick water
breaching
the thin blue air   as if
    nothing more important
might be imagined
than to touch
the entire world

with its being

Shelling

He is shelling, armed
with a small blue pail and a pair
of long-handled tongs.
He does not have to bend
to pluck them from the sand,
but can lift them
without ever touching
their rough beauty, their wet
brininess. I feel for him
a peculiar pity
as he pushes the plastic grab
into the damp sand, and hauls
another up, oblivious
to their many small deaths,
    not stooping
to understand their brokenness,
    not taking them up
one at a time, gratefully
into his hand.

Oyster Shell

It so closely resembles
the black petrified foot
of some seabird,
that I cringe
at its stony dismembered webs,
sharp bony ridges
where the toes should be,
one end upswept
into the stumpy imitation
of some long-dead reptilian leg.
How easily
in a world open to interpretation,
the tensile mind
curls itself
around every possibility.

Curiosity

This morning…a gull
walking the beach beside me
like a small feathered dog,
tethered only
by the invisible leash
of curiosity.

Scrabble

See how they come,
crawling up the beach,
foam-tipped fingers erasing
the masterpiece of their last rising
and beginning, once more
to rearrange the little words
of the sand. Unencumbered
by any weight of syntax or grammar,
they deftly stir last night's conclusions
into the complexities of another sunrise
and achieve,
for a few short hours,
a kind of blind equilibrium
in the undulating brim
and ebb
of the tide.

Gift

As always,
I would bring you
something . . . some sea-gift
of sun-whitened shell
curling into itself
like a stone flower, smooth
and lustrous . . . sacred
with the imprint
of one brief, yet anonymous life;
unlike . . . but not so unlike
the lives we live, chambered
yet reaching, as we make
of ourselves, a proper gift
to each other.

Precipice

I'm still numb with sleep
but in the world outside,
light and sound are weaving
disparate strands
into the fabric of another day.
The Burlington Northern rumbles
through town, pouring its lonely whistle
over the countryside; the percussion
of wheel against steel, a rhythm
underlying everything else
for miles around.
Nothing is certain yet.
If I rise from my chair, all may be lost.
This moment may fly apart
like warm glass shatters
in a sudden cold. Every morning
is a precipice…a stepping-off.
What I wouldn't do
to hold a single moment captive
in my hands.

Until We Come

Her blue Danish Christmas plates,
The ones I always admired,
Hang on *my* wall now, while she
Lingers on in the nursing home,
Drowsing away mornings in front of the TV,
Listening as Kenny-down-the-hall
Calls for his long-lost sister, and
Waiting out the long afternoons
Until we come…all smiles…to ask
How her day was, and how she feels.
Always the same questions
Because it's hard to know what to say
When you are free-as-a-bird,
With nothing more in mind
Than to get home again as soon as you can,
Away from the heavy portent
Of frail bodies and unpleasant smells,
To your own little universe
Where her plates are hanging, so blue
Against your wall.

Glass Tumblers

They number six.
Deep-cupped. Gold-rimmed.
Their pressed-glass sides rippled
with concentric circles, nubbed
with leaves. Lip-rubbed, until
once-bright rims attained
a mellow transparency, they speak
late-night dinners around
farmhouse tables. Work-lined faces
bowed over simple food.
The land, turning
beneath the hard-shouldered plow
of will. And life
poured out
one glassful at a time.

Patina

Each object
is a world unto itself,
smoothed beneath hands long-forgiven
their human frailty. Pummeled
by storms of temperament or weather,
we love this mute evidence
of lives which came and went like us
and likely did the best they could
with what they were given,
the dry seasons interspersed
with the damp.

Willy-nilly
for Gary and Sandra

Back then, it was always afternoon.
The sun was always hot, and my arms
were always sunburnt
and speckled with brown.
You were there. Sandra, too.
And we roamed the grassy bottoms
under the slow gaze
of the neighbor's cows,
letting the afternoon take us
willy-nilly
wherever butterflies flashed yellow
from one clump of sweet-clover
to the next.
Back at the house, Aunt Velma
leaned over her stove, frying chicken.
And life was really that good.
We were really loved that much.

Sun-rapt, oblivious
in a world of our own,
we would shake off shoes and socks,
step into the minnowed heaven
of the creek, and stand long
in its dappled coolness, giggling
as tiny silver fishes
nibbled at our feet.

Three Appaloosa Mares

Three Appaloosa mares
are grazing at mid-pasture, lipping
the long blades of late summer grass. They drowse
in the mid-day sun . . . nose-to-tail . . . swatting flies.
From the roadside, they might be
a mounded dish of vanilla ice cream,
dotted all over with chocolate chips.

The stallion
watches them hungrily
from the bottomless brown
of his eyes.

County Farm

There is no barn
where cats stand, tails up
in an eager circle, waiting
for steaming milk fresh-poured
from a brimming pail.

No pigeons
cooing in the loft, or horses
down below shaking halters,
whinnying for oats,
stomping impatient hooves.

No pigs, fattening to market.
No bull to taunt in the pasture.
No stubborn pony named Nancy
to buck you off
on the way to school.

No one stirs the cream corn,
hulls beans in the steamy old kitchen,
or lifts old folks
from their once-a-week bath
in the claw-foot tub.

That big white house,
so full of sorrow and hard work,
love and good humor,
has long-since tumbled down,
been plowed under, and planted to corn.

An entire generation
has simply vanished, turned over
into the dark Iowa soil.

All that remains now
are an open field, a few dreary lines in
"The History and Government of Sac County"
and my mother's stories,
which go on telling themselves
in me, transplanted
into the fertile loam of my life,
and reaping
a bountiful harvest.

Doing the Dishes

I wanted to wipe,
because whoever washed
had to deal with
the cold gray lumps of oatmeal
floating in the half-filled pan of water,
suspended in it . . . stickily . . . since breakfast
like so many globs of library paste, waiting all day
for us to come home from school
and clean it up.
                    You wanted to wipe
because you were my little brother,
and wanted to do everything
I wanted to do.

We argued over it
unabated
through years of green army men
and butterfly collections,
Boy Scouts and sleepovers,
church camp and first dates.

I guess we were normal.

Even now,
as my sink fills with sudsy rainbows,
a little angst
rises up from the water
to remind me of you.

Mother

I see
how she breathes
through the pores of my skin,
whispering her story
into the world's ear, playing me
like an instrument. I tell her
my life is my own, but she knows better.
We are two women sleeping
under the blanket of one body.
My toes tap to her rhythm.
They want to dance, like she did.
My hands are her hands, big-knuckled
with sinuous blue veins
I wish would disappear, but won't.
With them, I touch the faces
of her great grandchildren, knowing
that she touches them too.
We are one experience now,
our many misunderstandings waving
a slow goodbye, growing smaller
    with distance.
I carry her forward, into the future.
And she is light, and wise, and brimming
with remembrance.

Waiting

There,
Just beyond
The dark trunks of trees,
Their tangled branches,
A pale pink light stands
Waiting.

Perhaps today,
If I am worthy,
If I remain quite still,
The shy yellow bird of the sun
Will come once more
To peck
From my outstretched hand.

Foxtail

If you watch them
   wave their shaggy
     seeded manes,

You may discern
   the spirit
     of the wind,

Whose language
   is the flutter and the flap
     of cottonwood and ash,

Whose silvered fingers
   softly stroke
     the tresses of the foxtail,

And transform
   the humblest fallow field
     into a vast and honeyed sea,

Restless as any
   gold-flecked ocean
     tossing in the light.

A Poem for Mary

You have made, of the world
A paper cup,
Holding in its heart
The vastness of oceans,
Blue and salty seas, complete
With labels and longitudes.
Now,
You can lift it easily
In your two human hands
And place it wherever
You want.

Gossips

Aspens
Whisper
Leaf to leaf
In a breeze just passing through.

They stand about
Like old women gossiping, leaning
    into each other,
And tease me with their pleasant chatter,
A language of leaf and air
I cannot understand.

What Harvest

for Arnold

He must watch now
While children and grandchildren
Plan and plant a spring garden,
Inter-lacing the pumpkins
With the tomatoes, poling up beans,
Pushing the soil aside in his name.
Lord-willing, he will thrive through summer
And reap what he could not sow himself.
Lately, losses have been piling up:
A long illness, the hospital, worried faces
Hovering over his. But today,
He went out to the barbershop.
He sat in the chair, and chewed the fat
With an old friend. What harvest
More bountiful than that?

A Life

A life is a spacious thing,
a creaking, sighing, singing thing.
A thing to be swept, and polished,
and rearranged at will. A life
is a shore, washed over and again
by the same gray-green waves,
but retaining none. A life is an invitation
to love, but not a demand for it.
A life is not a possession,
nor is it an obligation, nor
is it a commodity to be traded,
though it often seems so.
A life resists imposed value.
It simply is. That
is its beauty.

What Remains

A week ago, in haste
we emptied her room
of its few possessions, not pausing
to notice the subtle heft
of long-used objects, or how
we rushed to decide
what to keep . . . what to let go.
Days have blurred by. She is resting now
in the grass-knit soil of South Dakota,
and we are back at life again,
quite compass-less without her,
sorting through the tangle
of what remains.

Already
her violets are lonely for her,
and I don't know how to sing them
back to life.

Owl

"Glory be to God for dappled things"
Pied Beauty, Gerard Manley Hopkins

No common glory
Sails the star-strewn night, to be
Unraveled by the light of morning, to
Seek refuge from it in the hollowed-out hands of God,
And dream its soft dream of rabbits, grateful for
Such a warm and breathing world, so dappled
With furry things.

At Last

Do trees ache
with the dead weight
of a lifetime's slow reach
for the sun? Do they dream
of one day falling, released from
heartwood's heavy burden, from
branches outspread, forever seeking
the unattainable?
Is the effort at last, and finally
too much for them, and do they
fall, relieved of the long shadows
of the years, to be sun-eaten,
sun-devoured, sun-filled, at last?
Do they ache, as we do,
with the
weight
of the God
inside our heads?

Disciples

Feet refreshed,
pierced
by his humility,
they still
do not quite understand
what he is about.
He has washed them
with hands
that have broken bread,
touched lepers, held children,
mixed mud
   to anoint blind eyes.
What impossible
depths of love
does he call them to
now?

Last Poem Before India

I
an elaboration of cells
huddled   in the warmth
of an eternal soul
traveling the universe
lacking in wisdom   but
brandishing life
weighing   measuring   assaying it
   curious of its mystery
   incredulous of its beauty
   aching with its cruelty
touching that which lies within my grasp
and leaving the rest   longing
to understand   once and for all
just who   and what
I am

Fly-by-night

Tonight
we split the indivisible sky
precisely
into two halves:
Above us, the pit
of bottomless space, hung
with numberless stars.
Below us, a slow-moving tapestry of lights,
scribbled over the dark slate of fields.
Between the two, a shifting veil
of wind-drifted cloud buoys us up
as it quivers, and dances
in the common
light.

Whatever Dreams

If a man must lie
on a mat, his face turned away from crowds
crossing the busy Delhi rail station,
is it dignity, or shame,
or simply the omnipresence of bony poverty
which averts the eyes
of every passer-by, and leaves him
folded alone
into whatever dreams he once had for himself,
to sleep away the night?

Petals, dropping

Petals, dropping
from the tall pink fountain
of the bougainvillea, descend
the long tangled stairway of its vine
and settle, softly
into the drab gray sand at its feet. They are so like
the sandaled, dark-eyed women
whose brilliant saris drift, like blossoms
down the narrow backstreets
of Delhi, one undeniable remedy
for all of the back-breaking dreariness
in life.

The Tooth Fairy

Four hundred rupees.
A small fortune
For holding two open spots
For the advent of two new teeth. But,
Not unusual in Delhi, where space
Is at a premium.

The Humblest of Threads

On the day that I was born,
a man took a pistol, and killed
Mohandas Gandhi
in the heart of this garden, a few short steps
from the little house
where he sat daily, spinning cloth
and peace
from the humblest of threads. Today, we arrive
from many cultures
to follow his painted footsteps to that spot,
taking sober measure
of the loss,
but we are not a hair's breadth closer
to the fulfillment of his dream.

Of Salt and Stars

Meteors
Sift down
The dark face of night
Like salt
Thrown over God's shoulder.
I wonder,
Have we made Him
Superstitious?

The Field

She stands among the ripened years, and waits
Like grain, sore-bent by every sigh of wind,
Anticipates the reaper's rhythmic bend
And swipe, the gathering-in of summer's sate.
She finds herself grown heavy with the dew
Of many dawns, the heat of many days,
And wonders why life's open-handed grace
Preserves her, though so many years accrue.
But, those of us who gather round her chair
As childhood memories animate her face,
Would listen, though she speak long into night
If only she would tell us how to bear
The bitter hardships we will never taste,
The burden of our all-too-easy lives.

The Fawn

That morning
I didn't notice how mist
Had crept up the stiff stalks
Of summer's last grasses,
Gathering light as it rose.

A few sleepy crickets
Still coaxed a little music
From world-weary thighs, and
Their songs filled the meadow,
But I paid no mind.

Somewhere along the horizon
A narrow moon paled, and
Sailed softly over night's edge
Like an apparition.
It was nothing to me.

But then…there you were!
Standing stock still, and perfectly wild
In a pool of deep shadow,
While a few gold leaves trembled
In the air above your head.

Something like a key turned inside me.

And I began to think
How God must ache for our gaze
When the sun stands up
Every morning, a perfect tower
Of light.

Soon!

Frost this morning. Shivers
of light from every
blade of grass. Milkweed pods
atop dry stalks, a few disheveled threads
of silk and seed
still hanging. Raspberry leaves
whispered in white. The sun
coming on…warming them. Geese aloft
in long clumsy V's, crying
"Soon! Soon!"
Who knew
there were so many shapes
and shades of brown?
Face cold…heart
happy.

Blessing

At an hour when air and field
and all that lies between
has brindled into half-darkness,
we pass two deer grazing
among the skeletal remains
of last year's corn. They do not look up
as we pass, but stand confident
in their near-invisibility
as the glare of our headlights
flares their eyes bright, then
moves on through the dark.
At the corner, we turn and are
soon home, swallowed-up again
by the ordinary.
And yet, some presence
lingers for hours
at the edge of my awareness,
as though a thick curtain
had parted, allowing the utterly
wild and unknowable
to walk through.

Dot to Dot

As I sprinkle unholy water
over the undisguised poverty of shirts
    you left behind;
as I press the hot iron to them, and the
bleach-laced scent of cotton rises;
just so, rises the sweet incense
    of our connection.
I remember you, baby boy:
architect of blocks and words, lover
of stories. These days, you ponder
dry and brittle truths, plumbing depths
I will never know, connecting
ever more complex dots.
When you speak, I silently vow
to get myself a dictionary. I buy
books on philosophy at the Goodwill,
read just enough to stay curious.
With each passing day,
I feel your life gather speed,
Moving away to the future.

It is what I always dreamed for you,
this distance . . . this leap.
If only I could come along.

One Small Gesture

Carefully, from the center
of the arrangement, I remove
the four red roses. They are perfect
in a way that words cannot capture,
each petal folded, like silk
into the velveteen purse of the bloom.
I wire their stems together
and hang them to dry
in the dark sarcophagus of my closet,
for I cannot bear to let them go just yet.
This one small gesture
unravels my every intention
to remember you safely, from afar.
In better years, you would cut
a single rose from your garden
and float it, fairy-like, in a crystal globe
on your dining room table.

You loved roses.

And you were not a woman
to relinquish them
until their last ounce
of fragrance and beauty
had been gleaned.

Equilibrium

There is joy so great
Your soul slips through your hands
That you might grasp it.

There is despair so deep
You beg your soul return,
A friendly face.

But where, pray tell
Is equilibrium?

Such Ties

Nested clutch of fallen leaves
wind-swept   snagged
at sidewalk's edge
what binds them
but the crisp tension
of touch
extending itself into
and through the others
even as we
are bound by such ties
though silken
and fragile as webs
we strengthen
each other

Some Days

Some days
I am fragile, and dry
As a winter-bit leaf
Blowing in the wind.

Some days
I am rooted…an oak,
A woman of few words
But many thoughts.

Some days
I fall…and other days
I rise up. Who
Can tell the difference?

Found Poem

Yesterday   impatience
cried-me-over
again
I couldn't quite be stuck
waiting all day
for years   the way
I did not deserve
feeling sad   again

Long moments
tenderness-I-remember
cried for yesterday
then
wrote me silence
it worked   I sent off life
came home   let the hurt
slide off my head

There I Was

One day
I went looking for myself.
I opened books, turned pages.
I was not there.
I lay back in the grass
and pondered the shape of clouds.
I was not there.
I overturned a stone in the garden.
Ants scattered everywhere,
but I was not there. I looked
into the faces of friends…found love,
but I was not there. I looked back
down the long string of days
that had been my life, but I was
no longer there.
I was so lonely for me. So, I sat
and I sighed, and I let it be.
I gave up on trying to find myself.
And what do you know?
There I was.

Channeling Lucille Clifton

All my love's a pondering
a thinking a
knowing
every nerve every cell
every hair on my head
alive   alive   alive
invisible god-thoughts
working clay kneading
soul clothing formlessness
so soft so breathless so
everything
the unseen need of you
in me   whispering
yes that's good
that's good

In the Mirror

Flash
of silvered brows
time-creased smile
eyes   staring back at me   seeing
what I did not allow myself
   some days
the loss-of-it   unbearable
not that I was
denied   but that
I kept myself
from it   believing
   others
more worthy

What Journeys

Fresh from dreams
from imaginings unwound
like thread
from a spool of light

no end no
beginning

What journeys
my fretful frivolous falling-over-the-
edge soul must have made
long white wings opening
and closing   fisted talons
gathering me
again and again
from dust

String Theory

Matter
Being a kind of silent symphony
Vibrating strings of energy
Pulsing   spinning   leaping
From one dimension to the next
Defying imagination
Stars
   Worlds
      People
         Pebbles
All madly dancing as one
No wonder
We dream of heaven   No wonder
We ache for God

Questioning the Moon

Pale moon. Lonely flier.
Little scoop chasing darkness,
Trailing light. Do you ever tire
Of the eternal cycle that is your life?

Still windless wanderer. Seducer of tides.
Sifter of the body's salty sea.
How many now are your
Wide and endless circles?

Have you seen how we hurry
Through this beautiful world,
Not noticing that it is beautiful?
That we, too, are beautiful?

Why is it, do you think,
That good and evil have become
A double-edged sword
Of our own wielding?

And, doesn't it seem
Such a long wait to be born
And then, a whole lifetime of
Learning how to live?

Anyway, little moon, I love the way
You soften our darkest midnight
With only the reflected fire
Of a single burning star.

Praises

You are a white fire,
the steep brilliance of stars,
the fragrance of lilacs
burning in spring, and unforgettable.
You are the jittering electricity
of thought, magnified into
planets, and solar systems, and galaxies.
You are the whisper of wings in the night,
and the soft answer to that whisper.
You are an amber-threaded honey,
hived and secret, sweet to the tongue.
From the threshold of infinity
you apprehend our smallest sigh, you pity
our deepest sorrow. You are
love's endless longing for itself.
And, as I said,
you are a white fire.

Footfall

Oh, the mist-winged
Slow-opening eye.
The streamered
Stealth-filled footfall
Of morning.
The pure, unassayed
Gold of it!

Haiku

long after sundown
one sad bird cries on and on
little stars bring light

time to light the lamp
shadows stand in the corners
chewing on secrets

old tomcat rumbles
the thunder of contentment
filling up the room

rain tapping on glass
my garden of tangled dreams
rising like new grass

Smiles

The plowed field
Lies bare as a peeled apple,
Its breath full of ghosts
Rising to catch the fading light.
Far off
A wailing train swallows steel
To the bright cities
While deer step out into moonlight,
Their hooves stamping smiles
In the soft earth.

Fall Planting

I laid them, wrapped in paper husks,
Into a damp and shallow grave,
Their bulbous hearts, a sacred trust

Assigned this bumbling garden knave.
I bid them sleep long winter's night
Whose bite undoes the proven brave,

With blossoms folded out-of-sight
Beneath the starkness of the snow.
How like a prayer, this sacred rite

Whose crowning, none but springtime knows:
The faith that draws them up from death
Into spritely, dancing, rainbow rows

And rouses again, the honeyed breath
Of warmer days, and creatures blest.

It So Happens

It so happens, that life
Is more complicated
Than I imagined. I want

To find a way to untangle
The knotted mystery
Of my own soul. However,

It seems
I am neither qualified, nor possessed
Of enough courage

By a longshot.

Trove

Within the symmetry of four straight walls,
Years of your living had deposited, silently
Layer on layer of detritus; an archeological dig
Of scattered unopened mail, yard sale finds,
Video tapes, out-of-date canned goods,
Clothes never worn . . . pictures never hung.
Radios long gone-silent. Silverware. Dishes.
Magazines. Even an American flag.
Every relic of a solitary life
Dropped, then systematically ignored
While your living-space shrank to a chair,
A color TV, an occasional night out.
   No matter. I loved you.
And I knew it was your trove, your hedge
Against death, and other unpredictables.

After you were gone,
I sifted for months through the ruins,
Like a prospector panning for gold
In the vast lonely river of life.

Boomers

In spite of resolutions
To the contrary,
We sit in coffee-lined circles
Comparing aches and pains,
Detailing old friends' surgeries, and hoping
Our own occasional twinge
Will yield to ibuprofen
Or a long-overdue change in diet.
Exercise becomes us...when we get it,
And the rest of the time
We work crosswords and Sudoku,
Coveting the tenuous life of the mind.
We whisper and snicker
At those who nip and tuck, daring
What the rest only dream.
Every day, the world
Becomes less and less our oyster.
Who knew we could be
So predictable?

Some Remembrance of You

In some distant day,
when I fall through
the frost-withered canopy
of time;
when, cell-by-cell, my body
embraces silence;
when what I have named
as mine disengages itself from me
and I rise, unfettered, from it;
I pray that some
remembrance of you
might pour, sweet and golden,
through me;
that the lies we told ourselves
might fade
into forgetfulness
and nothing remain
but love.

Electric

I touch quiet
the bridled energies
surging behind the wall.
Light flees the room
and darkness swallows me whole.
Inside my body, blood whispers
heart to hand…hand to heart,
lulling me to sleep.

How casually we disappear
into the extinguished light,
careless of currents still
sparking within us.

In dream
some unnamed life,
hived and humming beneath the skin,
paces and waits
for touch
to flash it bright.

Whatever

Whatever the condition
Of my heart…one small brown cricket
Still sings beneath the step.
The dark night
With its unfeeling stars,
Turns over to morning again,
And I am satisfied.

Again

Dogwoods
Flare up, blood-red
From the tangled trenches
Of winter.

Their roots run deep
Into the roughage
Of last summer's
Grasses. Again,

The broad white
River of snow
Has begun its long
Surrender to the rain.

Every year it is the same.

Some things die
That others
May be reborn.

Eagle Nesting

Unmoving,
head beneath wing,
she does not tear flesh
nor soar updrafts
nor pierce with yellow eyes the life
  of any tender prey,
but broods
within the tangled circle
of a snow-walled nest.
Talons in-curled
fierceness deferred
achingly *maternal*,
she covets the quickening
  of three small eggs,
denying winter its bite
by the hollow-boned
grace
of her wings.

Tulips

Tulips, tumbled together
in the pink pitcher, have lingered
there a full week, lengthening
and stretching into the days,
swaying imperceptibly
to the rhythm and bend of
light and dark, the soundless
dance of sun…moon…stars.
Each morning I notice
some transformation in them,
some change of attitude. Today
two yellows dip their faces
below the container's glass rim,
the curvature of their stems, a green grace.
Pinks and whites stand erect,
open-mouthed and receptive,
blindly hopeful of bees.
And then, there is the one
white-lipped beauty
thirsting after innocence, that leans
far out into the light brimming
at the east window,
and silently drinks
the pale blue tea of morning.

Repetition

Isn't life simply
A repetition
Of the same beautiful phrase,
Rearranged and spoken
Again and again?

The blue expanse of the sky
Smiles up at itself
From the pond's glassy face.

Birdsong echoes birdsong
In the misty distances
Of morning. The silent stars

Keep on lobbing their light
Back and forth, forever
Across the depths of the universe.

And who among us can gaze
Into a grandchild's eyes
And not find, reflected there

The faint, but sure cognition
Of his own limitless soul?

Now That She's Four

Her perfect eyebrows
rise and fall
with dramatic effect,
the frill and flutter of eyes unable
to disguise their obvious mischief.
What is she up to now?
What spark undoes
her every intention to hide it?
She knows I know, and that is half the fun.
We are co-conspirators, she and I,
our eyebrows arching-as-one
as we each try to guess
what the other
is thinking.

Buttercup

Lately renamed Ella Rosemarie

Before I had any solid notion of her,
she rounded into dream
and grasped my finger, the connection
a sure one. I covet her coming
in the knowledge that she is likely
to be the last. If I could, I would
reach out as she is born, and catch her
in my hands.
What will we be like, together?
Will she love me?
How much time will we have?
I want her to know how important love is,
how it warms the body, and also the soul.
I want to giggle with her, and share secrets.
I want to paint her toes.

I want to stand behind her, at the swing
Unable to resist her cries of
"Higher! Higher!"

Believing

It is spring . . . just barely,
and already, like a child
I have lost my gloves
for want of wearing them.

Through the cold enumeration
of days, my fingers go numb
but I bear it, refusing to
consider a replacement,
or the implied security
of a length of twine stretched
cuff-to-cuff
through my sleeves.

Unruly . . . devil-may-care,
I walk bare-fisted
into the world, believing.

What There Was

Wind, soughing in pines.
Skitter of leaves, on asphalt.
Snare drum of chickadee.
Trees, still brave with apples,
    rust above…rust beneath.
Rapture of birdsong.
Maples, popping red against blue.
No pussy willows, as yet
    but this:
Cloudless curve of sky.
Sunlight, warm on my hair.
The faint ticking of snowbanks
    as they melt.

A few small
But significant
Joys.

A Pair of Wild Swans

White on white,
I barely notice them
crossing the milk-colored sky
pale wings pumping
long necks reaching
as they sail
over snow-muffled fields,
careless of bitter mid-March winds,
the bite of sleet,
or any other thing
than to move with purpose,
long white wings folding and unfolding
to the siren call
of a pond not-yet-open,
a nest
not-yet-built.

Good Karma

A deer has crossed the road, just there,
where the dismal foam of old snow
slumps into the ditch. The treehouse

is open for business, but has no takers
yet. As I turn the far corner, the old
brindled dog runs out and growls, but

thinks better of it, and walks me home.
Some idiot has dumped a microwave
where the tiny wild strawberries grow.

But even so, the afternoons unwind
like fingered beads beneath my touch,
each one round, and perfect in its right.

In the garden, irises spear green through
a rat's nest of damp leaves. With enough
good karma, they just might bloom by May.

All For Me

Some brightness
called me to watch
as ice-beaded branches
filled with sunrise,
each bead, a tiny sun
bending light into rainbow
as it warmed and liquefied,
as it surrendered stillness
to the rapture of falling.

This moment . . . this.
All for me.

The feeling
poured off me
as if it were visible.

About the Author

Sharon K Sheppard has been writing poetry for over 30 years. Her roots are set firmly in the midwestern states of Iowa, South Dakota, and Minnesota. She enjoyed a long and happy career in the paper industry. Sharon is the grateful mother of two sons, and grandmother to four children who never stop surprising her. She resides with her husband in Isanti, Minnesota.

Made in the USA
Charleston, SC
27 September 2014